*signature licks*

# BILLY JOEL CLASSICS
## 1974-1980

by Robbie Gennet

**The Recording**

The accompanying CD contains full-band demos with featured keyboard parts isolated on the right side of the stereo mix. Keyboard parts that warrant closer attention are played alone as slow demos where shown.

Warren Wiegratz: Keyboards and Saxophone
Doug Boduch: Guitars
Tom McGirr: Bass
Scott Schroedl: Drums

Recorded, Mixed, and Mastered by
Jim Reith at Beathouse Music, Milwaukee, WI

Cover photo by Neal Preston/CORBIS

ISBN 0-634-02153-2

HAL•LEONARD®
CORPORATION

7777 W. BLUEMOUND RD. P.O. BOX 13819 MILWAUKEE, WI 53213

Visit Hal Leonard Online at
**www.halleonard.com**

# CONTENTS

# INTRODUCTION
## Billy Joel: A Brief Biography

Billy Joel is a classically trained pop composer who has many multi-platinum records and hit singles to his name. His songs have struck a chord with a widespread audience of all ages, and New Yorkers in particular have latched on to his localized characters and stories. This book/CD will break down some of the most memorable moments of his work in the seventies and early eighties, a period of great creativity during which he produced some of his most timeless and successful songs.

A native of Long Island, Joel began playing professionally in his teenage years, doing session work for producer George "Shadow" Morton. His most notable session of the time was on "Leader of the Pack" by the Shangri-La's. Joel also performed with a string of original bands and eventually dropped out of high school to concentrate on his budding musical career. After a few records with his band the Hassles, Joel regrouped a duo under the name Attila, playing a heavy, organ-based brand of psychedelic rock—a far cry from the music for which he would come to be known. Signed to Epic, Attila didn't find the success Joel had hoped for, and he fell into depression. After a few years, Billy signed a new record deal and came out with his solo debut, 1971's *Cold Spring Harbor*. Though his tour was well received, he was unhappy with the record and having trouble with his label. In 1972, he moved to Los Angeles and spent most of the year playing lounge piano under the name Bill Martin.

By the beginning of 1973, Joel had married his long-time girlfriend and was touring again. During this time, a Philadelphia radio station started playing a live version of "Captain Jack," and suddenly record labels were knocking on his door. After signing with Columbia, he recorded and released his major-label debut, *Piano Man*, which peaked the following year at #27 and garnered his first Top 40 hit with the title track, an ode to his time spent in the piano bar. His second album, 1974's *Streetlife Serenade*, reached the Top 40 as well and featured songs such as "The Entertainer" and "Root Beer Rag." In the midst of his rising popularity (and the first batch of many music industry awards to come), his growing dissatisfaction with California found him moving back east to his true hometown, New York City.

With new management on board, Joel released the self-produced *Turnstiles* in 1976, featuring the semi-autobiographical "Say Goodbye to Hollywood" and his paean to the Big Apple, "New York State of Mind." Though *Turnstiles* didn't fare well commercially, Joel was honing his craft as a songwriter and was about to unleash his biggest album yet. He teamed with legendary producer Phil Ramone and released *The Stranger* in the fall of 1977. Within months, it went to #2 and sold millions. Besides the classic ballad "Just the Way You Are"—Record and Song of the Year at the 1979 Grammys—the album also featured the Top 20 hits "Movin' Out (Anthony's Song)," "She's Always a Woman," and "Only the Good Die Young." Joel enlisted Ramone again for the follow-up album, *52nd Street*. Released in the fall of 1978, it spent eight weeks at #1 in the U.S. and sold over two million copies within a month of its release. *52nd Street* won Grammys for Album of the Year and Pop Male Vocal in 1980, while pop radio made hits of "My Life," "Big Shot," and "Honesty." Joel was not always the critics' darling, but his legions of fans and multi-platinum record sales more than made up for it. In fact, in 1979 Columbia Records named him their biggest-selling solo artist of the 20th century, with sales of *The Stranger* and *52nd Street* then totaling over 9 million units.

Joel followed the two hit records with his hardest-rocking album yet, the punk- and new wave-tinged *Glass Houses*, released in 1980. It would go on to reach #1 and stay there for six weeks, winning a Grammy for Best Rock Vocal Performance, as well as an American Music Award for Album of the Year and the People's Choice Favorite Male Pop Performer. "It's Still Rock 'n' Roll to Me" was Joel's first #1 hit and his biggest single to date. "You May Be Right," "Don't Ask Me Why," and "Sometimes a Fantasy" all hit the Top 40 as well. He followed up *Glass Houses* with his first live record, *Songs in the Attic*, which focused solely on earlier material. Live versions of *Say Goodbye to Hollywood* and *She's Got a Way* became Top 40 hits, and *Songs in the Attic* became Billy's fourth consecutive Top 10 album.

Soon after *Songs in the Attic* was released, Joel suffered a broken wrist in a motorcycle accident and went through a painful divorce. His next album, *The Nylon Curtain*, didn't sell as well as its predecessors, though critics were warming up to him. Big radio hits like "Pressure" and "Allentown" were also featured on the newly blossomed MTV. *An Innocent Man* soon followed, reaching #4 in 1983. Nominated for an Album of the Year Grammy, it generated six Top 40 singles, including three that reached the Top 10: "Uptown Girl" (#3), "Tell Her About It" (#1), and "An Innocent Man" (#10). By 1985, Joel had enough hits to fill a two-volume *Greatest Hits* collection, featuring two new singles: "You're Only Human (Second Wind)"—his eighth Top 10 hit—and "The Night Is Still Young." *Greatest Hits* sold over 20 million copies in the U.S. alone, cementing Joel's status as a pop icon.

Billy's next album of new music was *The Bridge*, which made the Top 10 in 1986, spawning the hits "Modern Woman," "A Matter of Trust," and "This Is the Time." Ray Charles, Steve Winwood, and Cyndi Lauper all appeared on the album in a rare spate of guest spots. Joel then became one of the first major Western artists to tour the USSR, recording his 1987 Leningrad performance for the live album "Kohuept" (Russian for *concert*). The next original album was his fourteenth for Columbia, the multi-platinum *Storm Front*, released in 1989. The #1 hit "We Didn't Start the Fire" was used in schools nationwide as a learning tool due to its fact-based historical lyrics. *Storm Front* reached #1, received numerous Grammy nominations, and also produced the hits "I Go to Extremes" and "Shameless" (which was very successfully covered by Garth Brooks). In 1990, the National Academy of Recording Arts and Sciences honored Billy Joel with a Grammy Living Legend award. After a four-year recording hiatus, Joel released *River of Dreams* in 1993. The album quickly reached #1, and the title track was a Top 10 hit. Four Grammy nominations followed in 1994, as well as certification that *Songs in the Attic* and *The Nylon Curtain* had hit the two million mark—moving Joel into a tie with the Beatles as the act with the most multi-platinum albums. Joel also became the only artist to have four albums—*52nd Street, Glass Houses, The Stranger*, and *An Innocent Man*—go septuple-platinum. In March, 1997, Joel received ASCAP's Founder's Award for lifetime achievement—joining the ranks of Paul McCartney, Bob Dylan, Leiber and Stoller, and other music legends. With worldwide sales of over 100 million units by 1999, Joel marked two more major milestones: in January he received the American Music Awards' Award of Merit, and in February he was inducted into the Rock and Roll Hall of Fame. In May of 2000 he was awarded an honorary Doctor of Music from Southampton College—one of many honorary degrees he has received.

As of this writing, *River of Dreams* is the last pop album Billy Joel has released. Since then, he has put out the live *2000 Years: The Millenium Concert* and 2001's classical endeavor *Fantasies and Delusions*. Both were well received by fans, who have also flocked to the Elton John/Billy Joel concert tours the two have undertaken. In 2001, Joel was honored by the Songwriter's Hall of Fame with the Johnny Mercer Award—their highest honor.

Billy Joel has been a long-time supporter of the Make a Wish Foundation (www.wish.org) and VH-1's *Save the Music* (www.vh1.com/insidevh1/savethemus).

# DISCOGRAPHY

The songs in this volume came from the following recordings:

*PIANO MAN.* "Piano Man," "Captain Jack"
Released November 1973            Produced by Michael Stewart and Billy Joel

*STREETLIFE SERENADE.* "The Entertainer," "Root Beer Rag"
Released October 1974            Produced by Michael Stewart and Billy Joel

*TURNSTILES.* "Say Goodbye to Hollywood," "New York State of Mind"
Released May 1976            Produced by Billy Joel

*THE STRANGER.* "Movin' Out (Anthony's Song)," "Just the Way You Are," "The Stranger,"
"She's Always a Woman," "Scenes from an Italian Restaurant"
Released September 1977            Produced by Billy Joel and Phil Ramone

*52nd STREET.* "Big Shot," "Honesty," "My Life"
Released October 1978            Produced by Phil Ramone and Billy Joel

*GLASS HOUSES.* "Don't Ask Me Why"
Released March 1980            Produced by Phil Ramone and Billy Joel

The sequence of producer credits shows Billy Joel's phase-out of Michael Stewart after two records. After Joel parted ways with Stewart, he produced *Turnstiles* alone. For *The Stranger,* he enlisted Phil Ramone as his engineer and eventual co-producer. The following two albums featured Ramone as the main producer, and it is Ramone's presence on the triumvirate of hit records that cements this time as a creative pinnacle in Joel's career.

# ABOUT THE AUTHOR

Robbie Gennet is a multi-instrumentalist, songwriter, and music journalist currently based in Los Angeles. Known primarily as a piano player, he has toured with rock bands such as Everclear, Seven Mary Three, and Saigon Kick on keyboards and guitar. He has won multiple "Best Keyboardist" awards in his home state, and has written a monthly column in *Keyboard* Magazine for the last four years. Along the way, Gennet has released a host of award-winning albums with various bands and solo.

Gennet has also written for *Keyboard*, *Gig*, and *Musician* magazines, and web sites including *MarsMusic.com* and *Musician.com.* He is currently performing both solo and with his bands Rudy and Rabbithead, as well as composing soundtrack music for film and television. Visit him online at *www.pianarchy.com.*

# PIANO MAN

**Words and Music by Billy Joel**

"Piano Man" could be Billy Joel's signature song, a paean to barroom piano players everywhere and an enduring hit in the Joel pantheon. This "story song" features different characters and their intertwining lives, regulars at the neighborhood bar where Joel's piano man leads them through their favorite songs. From the opening line—"It's nine o'clock on a Saturday; the regular crowd shuffles in"—Joel sets the scenario of all these disparate people coming together to share in "a drink they call loneliness." He reminds us that "it's better than drinking alone," alluding to the sometimes-temporary camaraderie that drinkers create. It is Joel's title character who leads them in song and brings them together "to forget about life for awhile." Joel even gives the piano man (himself) hope when the regulars who "put bread in [his] jar" ask him, "Man, what are you doing here?" As Joel can attest, there can be a career in piano beyond the barroom.

## Figure 1—Intro

The first two measures of "Piano Man" present a seemingly ad-libbed bit of riffing that adds to the song's piano-bar feel. The 4/4 time signature here is just a formality, as the section is meant to be played freely.

The main theme and verse progression start at measure 3, as the chords begin their descending waltz-style progression in 3/4 time. Instead of playing a straight "oom–pa–pa" waltz pattern here, Joel varies the duration of bass notes and chords subtly and adds interest while avoiding a cliché. The bass line descends straight down the C major scale for almost a full octave. Joel harmonizes this bassline with mostly primary triads (C, F, and G). The D7 chord at measure 9 is the first real surprise. The D7 serves as the V7 of V, and strengthens the movement to the V chord (G), which in turn resolves back to the root chord (C).

Measure 17 introduces the song's signature line, a repeating four-measure pattern with C arpeggios interspersed between chords.

Fig. 1

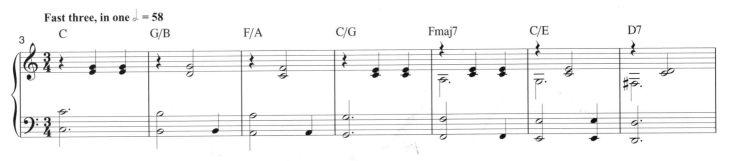

## Figure 2—Verse 1 and Verse 2

The chords in the verse start out the same as the descending progression of the intro (now played in more of a straight-ahead waltz fashion to support the vocals), with the very small exception of a D in the seventh measure (instead of a D7). Joel then fleshes out his chords with some added 9ths and a G9sus chord in measures 13–14.

The two verses are separated by a brief harmonica interlude, played over a variation of the verse pattern, then the crescendo on C and F/C in measures 23–26, in which the accordion enters to add to the more rollicking second verse.

The chord progression in the second verse is essentially the same, but Joel's vocal melody soars an octave higher, registering great emotional impact. Notice the well-used G/B (meas. 42) acting as a conduit to the A minor chord that begins the interlude.

Fig. 2

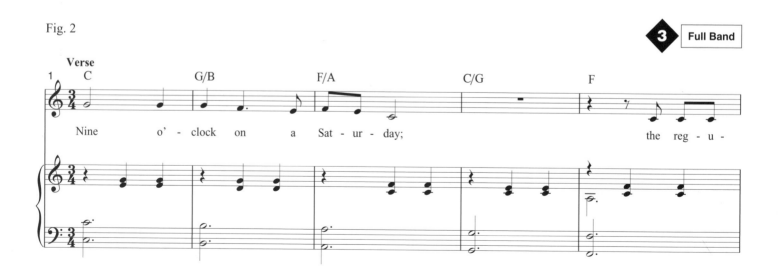

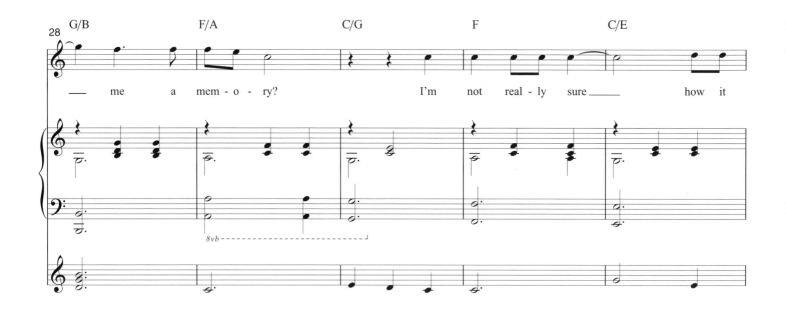

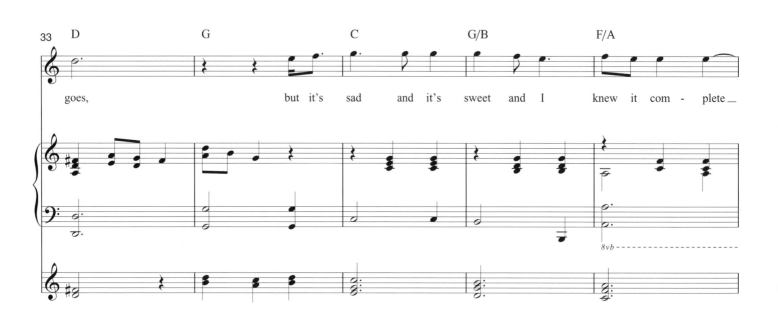

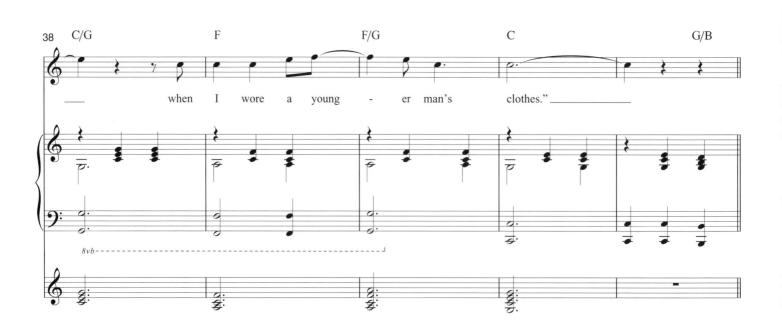

**Figure 3—Interlude**

The interlude serves as a transitional buildup to the sing-along chorus. Joel leads us down the A minor scale to F via a well-placed D/F♯ passing chord (meas. 3). However, the next time he uses it (meas. 7), instead of going to an F, he drops the bass note to make it a root position D major chord, the V of V, which he engages to resolve to the V chord (G). The last four measures of the interlude find our bass notes descending straight down the C major scale to the ultimate release of the tonic chord in the chorus. The overall effect is one big release of tension to the root chord of the chorus. Play the last four measures as a crescendo, building up intensity for the main hook.

Fig. 3

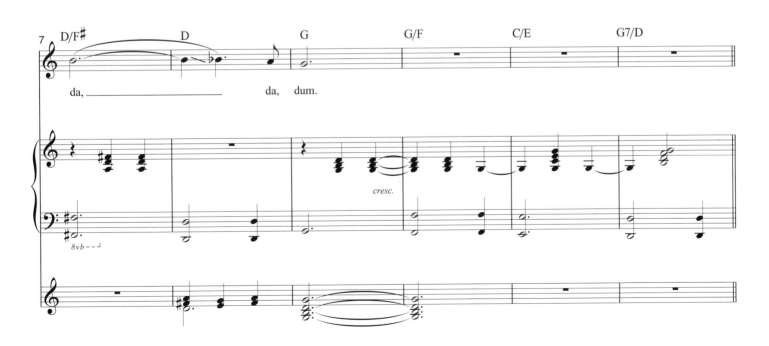

## Figure 4—Piano Solo

The story continues through variations of chorus, interlude, verse, and interlude. Then Joel takes a piano solo over a progression similar to the interlude, ultimately setting up a big chorus before the last verse. The solo is constructed of strong lines primarily based on chord tones. Of particular interest is his bluesy playing over the D chord at measure 3 (the F–F♯) and the Am/G chord at measure 6 (the E–E♭–D).

Fig. 4

# CAPTAIN JACK

**Words and Music by Billy Joel**

"Captain Jack" is an early Billy Joel narrative about a teenage loner living on the fringes of New York City. Joel captures the essence of a young man with too much time on his hands and no clear idea of his future, placing the lyrics in the second person so the listener becomes the subject. "Captain Jack" is either a drug or the dealer who brings it, and the artificial escape from a "one-horse town" never fills the emptiness inside. The protagonist has "everything"—cool clothes, a brand new car, a girlfriend—yet is never satisfied, and he tries to fill his hollow heart with drugs and seedy hangouts. But ultimately, though he hasn't found the answers to his emptiness, he sees it all coming to an end in the line, "Well, you're twenty-one and still your mother makes your bed, and that's too long." Joel's story is one to which most people can relate: the feeling that in our teen years, nobody truly understands us because in reality, we don't understand ourselves. "Captain Jack" is a timeless story that resonates decades after its inception. As long as there are teenagers struggling with self-discovery, "Captain Jack" will remain a poignant story and song.

### Figure 5—Intro

The first two measures of the intro (played on pipe organ) are comprised of a 16th-note figure in the right hand and a simple line in the left that implies the noted chord structure in the key of G. (This brief statement in G might seem odd now, but Joel is foreshadowing the chorus.) The C chord in measure 2 acts as a *pivot chord* (a chord present in two keys): the IV in G, and the V in F. When the piano enters in measure 3, he oscillates between the I and IV chords (F and B♭).

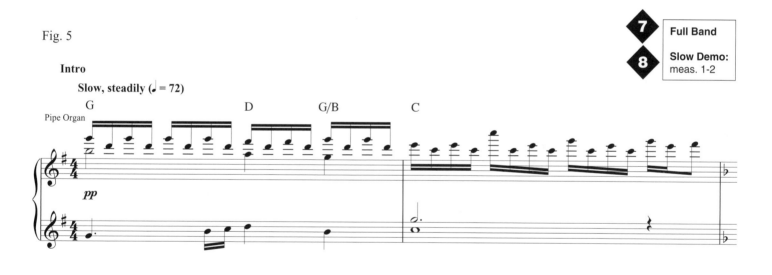

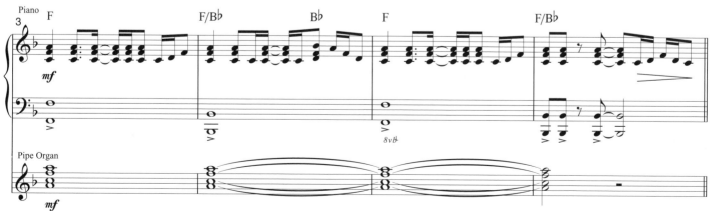

**Figure 6—Verse**

In the first five measures of the verse, Joel continues the I–IV–I movement. He uses a B♭maj7 the first two times, then switches up the change with a transitory Bm7♭5 to an unadorned B♭ chord in measure 6. He then drops from the IV chord (B♭) to the iii7 chord (Am7), and then moves to the V chord (C) to set up the return to the I chord (F). The next eight-measure verse works much the same, with two notable exceptions: first, Joel discards the Bm7♭5 for a simpler B♭(add9) in the third line; second, in the last bar, he moves from the Am to a D, a setup for the key change to G major in the chorus. Keep in mind that Am–D–G is a ii–V–I progression in G Major, a strong progression that works well in a transitional section.

Fig. 6

**9** Full Band

14

## Figure 7—Chorus

The chorus is comprised mostly of the I, IV, and V chords in G major. Notice at the end of measure 1 how Joel uses the G with the 3rd in the bass (G/B) to lead into the C chord, a common technique in his bag of tricks and an effective way to generate motion in a progression.

Fig. 7

**10** Full Band

Cap - tain Jack __ will get you by __ to - night, __

just a lit - tle push 'n' you'll be smil - in'. __

# THE ENTERTAINER

**Words and Music by Billy Joel**

In "The Entertainer," Joel tells of the highs and lows of being in show business. He traces the steps in rising to fame, but leads to the fact that without a hit, you can quickly disappear. No matter what the genre or decade, the sentiments Joel expresses ring true in an increasingly corporate game that often depends on expendable artists and ever-changing trends. The song's epic feel and complex arrangements seem to defy the corporate music scene.

## Figure 8—Intro

"The Entertainer" begins with this bright, syncopated melodic statement played on synth above a sprightly strummed acoustic guitar part. The piano plays a closely related part with simple harmonies in G. The synth is played with a slight portamento or "glide" setting to make each note slide into the next.

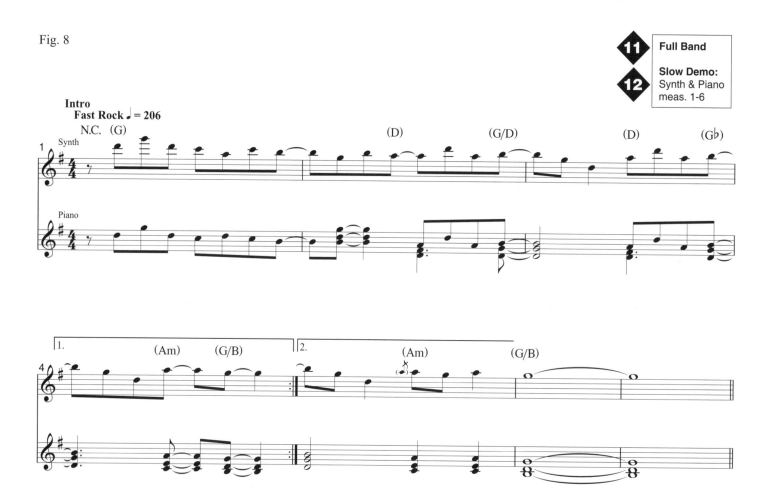

## Figure 9—Verse 3 and Interlude

Joel accompanies his voice on piano only in certain verses. The third verse is the first and simplest appearance of piano accompaniment—just full chords hit on the syncopated changes. The verse's construction begins with three symmetrical four-measure phrases, then a five-measure phrase added at the end, making a total of seventeen measures per verse (instead of the anticipated sixteen). The interlude is a synth/piano riff reminiscent of the intro.

Fig. 9

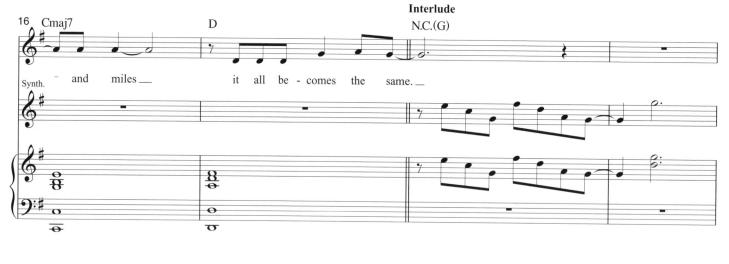

## Figure 10—Verse 5

This is the most involved verse, pianistically speaking. The piano begins with a two-measure lead-in to the verse, and already shows the bluesy direction we're headed. Joel plays an invigorating boogie-woogie piano part that would sound like an all-out solo if not for the vocal.

Fig. 10

**15** Full Band

**16** Slow Demo: meas. 1-19

# ROOT BEER RAG
**Music by Billy Joel**

Billy Joel is best known for his pop and rock songs, but "Root Beer Rag" stands out as a rare instrumental. Joel created a credible ragtime piece that hearkens back to the days of Scott Joplin and James P. Johnson. "Root Beer Rag" is in the key of C major, and has a very clear and cohesive structure.

**Figure 11—Intro and Theme**

The intro is a two-measure pattern (the C–C/B–F/A–F progression) that is played twice. The eight-measure theme is somewhat repetitive as well. If we break the theme into two four-measure sections, we see the first two measures of each of those sections are the same, using the C, B♭, and F chords. However, the final two measures of the theme contain a unique progression, complete with secondary dominants. Here's a run down: The F (IV) moves to D/F♯ (V of V), which resolves deceptively to C/G (we expect G). Next, Joel emphasizes the D in the last measure by preceding it with its dominant, A7 (V7 of ii). The D as stated here has no 3rd, but later in the piece it contains an F♯, demonstrating that Joel treats it too as a *secondary dominant*—the V of V.

Fig. 11

**17** Full Band

**18** Slow Demo: meas. 1-12

### Figure 12—Variation

This eight-measure section is a variation of the original theme. Here Joel moves the right hand up an octave and adds some exciting rhythmic anticipations, as in the ends of measures 2, 4, and 6. As expected in a variation, the harmony remains virtually unchanged, and here the last two measures of the interlude are in fact very similar to the last two measures of theme, except that now the D/F♯ is clearly thought of as F♯dim7, and the D7–G7–C progression at the end is clearly delineated by fully articulated chords.

Fig. 12

**19** Full Band

**20** Slow Demo
meas. 1-8

## Figure 13—Secondary Theme and Interlude 1

The first eight bars of this section demonstrate Joel's understanding of harmonic logic and planning. On the surface, we hear beat-by-beat changes of harmony, filled with secondary dominants over a descending bass line. But if we listen more closely, the first part is a four-measure phrase in F, divisible into two independent *phrase fragments* (subdivisions of a phrase). These phrase fragments are linked by the C7 in measure 2. The first cadence on the tonic (F) occurs at the end of the second phrase fragment, in this case, at the end of the phrase itself. The next phrase (meas. 5–8) is a restatement of the previous phrase, but now transposed up and played in the tonic key, C. Joel continues in measure 9 with new material and a dramatic break before wrapping things up in measures 15–16.

Fig. 13

**21** Full Band

**22** Slow Demo: meas. 10-16

*Play lower notes w/.L.H.

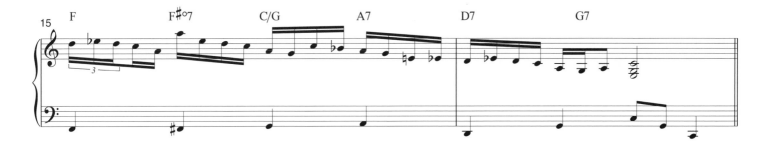

## Figure 14—Interlude 2

In this interlude section, Joel plays staccato *dyads* (two-note "chords") over a loosely implied dominant/tonic chord progression. In measure 4, he intensifies the texture by breaking up the basic pattern between the hands in a more syncopated fashion. Joel employs a chromatic descent in the chord progression, leading us down to an A7. The last two measures are true to the theme's harmony.

Fig. 14

**Figure 15—Bridge**

This section in A minor, the relative minor of the tonic (C major), begins a typical minor progression over a descending bass line. Joel creates most of the musical interest here through his inventive but stylistically appropriate rhythms.

Fig. 15

**24** Full Band

**25** Slow Demo: meas. 10-12

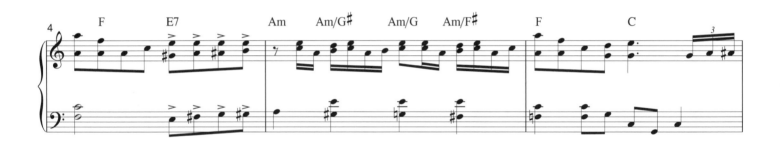

*Play lower notes w/ L.H.

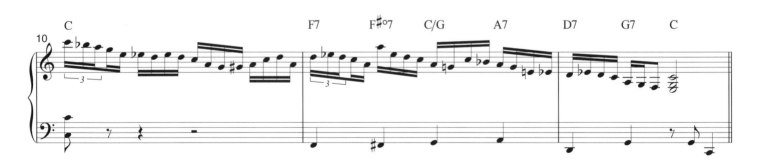

# SAY GOODBYE TO HOLLYWOOD

**Words and Music by Billy Joel**

Billy Joel has always been known as a quintessential New York songwriter, though he has his forays into the west-coast lifestyle in songs such as "Los Angelenos" and "Say Goodbye to Hollywood." The "goodbye" here is not just to the city itself, but also to old friends and lovers who don't stick around for long. Hollywood has always been used as a symbol of all that the city embodies, from greed and ego to fame and fortune. In a town full of fleeting moments, the bright lights and dirty streets are just a backdrop to the characters who come and go.

**Figure 16–Verse (Second Half) and Chorus**

This melancholy song is in C, and doesn't often venture outside the key. Throughout, Joel plays heavy eighth-note repetitions of the chords on top of a left-hand bass line in octaves, over an early rock-style beat—complete with castanet flourishes—that echoes Billy's early session work with the Shangri-La's. The verse chords outline a basic I–IV progression. An extra "breather" measure of F that appeared in the first half of the verse (not shown here) is not repeated; rather, measure 4 is truncated and launches us right into the chorus.

The chords used in the chorus are more adventurous, as evidenced by Joel's starting on the ii chord (Dm7) and his the use of colorful harmonies, such as the Dm7/G instead of a G or G7. He also avoids the tonic for eight measures, substituting the vi chord (Am) in its place, and creating an unsettled feeling.

Fig. 16

26 Full Band

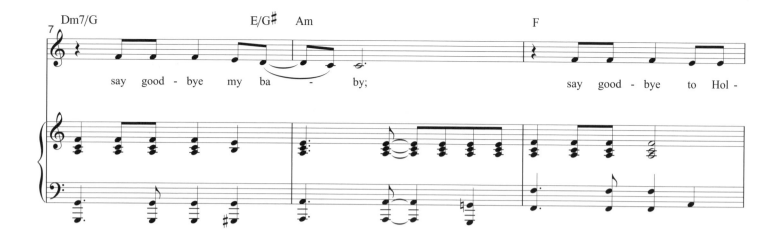

## Figure 17—Bridge

After a short reiteration of the simple and centered verse, Joel moves into the wandering chords of the bridge. The surprising B chord is the V of iii, and Joel resolves it to Em as expected. The D chord (V of V) in measure 7 "wants" to move to the V chord (G), but Joel instead jumps back to the I chord (C). The Dm–G played under the repeated word "forever" (meas. 15–16) underscores the melancholy feeling of the vocals beautifully.

Fig. 17

**27** Full Band

# NEW YORK STATE OF MIND

**Words and Music by Billy Joel**

Billy Joel is a New Yorker to the end, and with "New York State of Mind," he has written an unofficial anthem for NYC and its millions of citizens. In the song, Joel tells us that although he has traveled the country from coast to coast, there's no place like home. In fact, Joel is happy with any reminder of the city, such as the New York Times or the Daily News, and whether supping in Chinatown or driving down Riverside Drive, it's all fine with him. His performance of "New York State of Mind" at the September 11th Memorial Concert further cemented this song's symbolic resonance with the city.

**Figure 18—Intro**

"New York State of Mind" begins with an eight-measure intro in Joel's piano-bar style, played freely. Though he starts off clearly in C, he surprises us in measure 4 with the A♭maj7/B♭—basically a ♭VII chord borrowed from C minor. The rest of the intro outlines a ii–V movement, in which the F/G functions as the V.

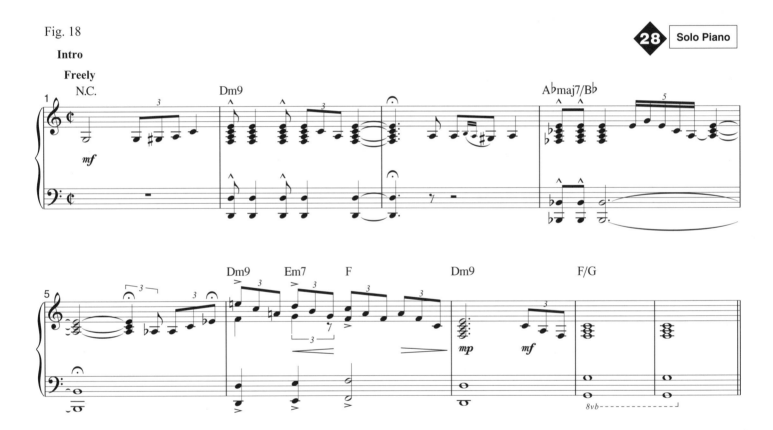

**Figure 19—Instrumental Verse**

This section acts as a second intro. Here Joel lays out the basic theme of the song: A beautiful, bluesy melody over what could be called an 18-bar blues. (Compare this progression to Ray Charles's "Hard Times.") Joel uses secondary dominants throughout, as many of the diatonic chords (Am, F, and Dm, for example) are preceded by their dominants (E7♯5, C7, and A7♯5, respectively). The B♭9 is the ♭VII chord (borrowed from C minor, and recalled from the intro); this chord contains the notes of an F minor chord (F A♭ C) and works great in sentimental settings like this one.

Fig. 19

**Verse**

**Slow Blues (Half-time feel)** ♩ = 60

**Figure 20—Bridge**

This bridge is the only real contrast to the eighteen-measure verses that abound in this song. Perhaps taking inspiration from the great Tin Pan Alley songwriters, Joel wisely avoids the compositional devices he used in the verse, both melodically and harmonically. The vocal line is broader rhythmically, yet falls in a tighter range. The chord progression is jazzier, with its frequent maj7 chords and wandering quality (moving from G to F to A, and back to G again before setting up another verse in C).

Fig. 20

## Figure 21—Outro

The outro presents a grand-sounding and dramatic close to an emotionally charged song. With held chords, solo flourishes, and wailing vocals, Joel sets up a fascinating ending. The final measures are filled with exciting harmonic twists, especially with the chords that follow the Bb9.

Earlier in the song, Joel resolved the Bb9 to C, but here (meas. 15–18) he resolves this secondary dominant to its I chord, Eb6, then follows with its IV chord, Ab, before jumping back to what amounts to a sophisticated and jazzy ii–V–I (C/D–Db13#11–D/C) progression in C. Basically, he is taking a trip around the circle of fifths leading back to the tonic: He moves from Bb to Eb to Ab, interrupts with the D, and then moves on to Db, finally ending on C.

A further note on the final four measures: The C/D in measure 17 chord functions as a ii chord, followed by the Db13#11, which functions as V; jazz players call this the *tritone substitution*, because it is a tritone away from the V chord. The D/C is a colorful way to end; the notes of the D chord sound as the 9th, #11th, and 13th of the C chord.

# MOVIN' OUT (ANTHONY'S SONG)

**Words and Music by Billy Joel**

In another of Joel's story songs, the main character Anthony is leaving home, motorcycle screeching as he tears off in search of a better life. Though the verses are written in the third person, Joel puts himself in Anthony's shoes in the chorus, personalizing the disillusionment and escapism in Anthony's struggle for independence. What is Anthony escaping? The status quo of working and living in his ethnic neighborhood for a house and a car just like all his neighbors. He asks, "Is that all you get for your money?" and follows with "It seems such a waste of time if that's what it's all about." Anthony's search for greater meaning in life is shared by most people transitioning from young, carefree teenagers into responsible adults, and the liberating roar of his motorcycle signifies a powerful—if temporary—escape from a "normal" life.

## Figure 22—Intro

The song starts out with simple right-hand chords played in steady eighths on piano, as the bass line, doubled by a lightly distorted guitar, gives contrasting rhythmic movement and leads us from chord to chord.

The song is in the key of D minor, and most of the chords are diatonic. The only chromatic exception in the intro is the E+, which Joel uses to link the C to the Fmaj7. The voice leading in the right hand is very smooth throughout, and the E+ makes it even more so.

Fig. 22

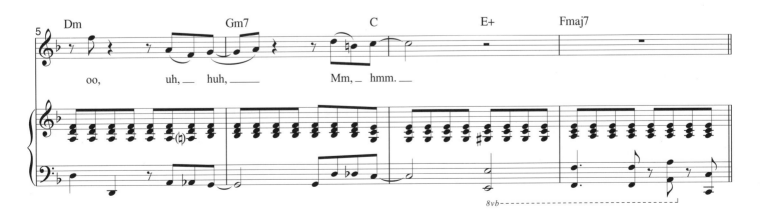

**35**

## Figure 23—Verse and Pre-Chorus

The verse is based on the progression established in the intro, but Joel makes some slight changes: He substitutes a C9sus for the plain C, an E7♭9 instead of E+, and a plain F triad for the Fmaj7. However, they function in the same way, which is important to notice and is corroborated by the bass line, which is essentially unchanged.

In measure 10, Joel dispenses with the right hand's insistent eighth-note rhythms, and lays down a whole note chord under the "heart attack-ack-ack-ack-ack-ack" line, one of more recognizable parts in the song.

The pre-chorus (meas. 17–23) serves as a setup to the title line, and lasts an uneven seven measures. The half-time feel and the three-note descending guitar figures create a downward spiral of sound that reflects Joel's rejection of middle-class values. The following eight-measure chorus (not shown) is essentially the same as the verse, with added woodwind parts and octaves in the bass line.

Fig. 23

**33** Full Band

**34** Slow Demo: meas. 16

**Figure 24—Outro**

It is here that we hear the revving of Anthony's motorcycle as he tears off and moves out, and this starts a musical ending and eventual fade. Joel jumps to the key of D major, giving an uplifting finale to the piece. This extreme variation of the main chord pattern becomes a majestic outro, complete with harmony lead guitar lines that double the piano melody.

Fig. 24

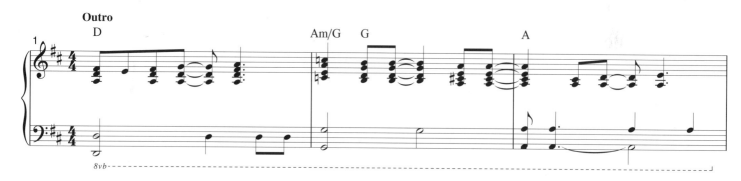

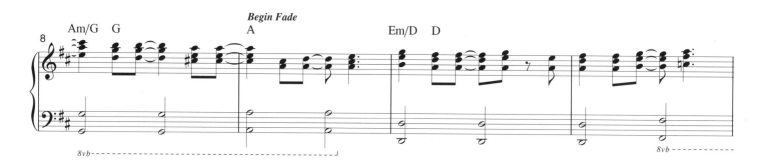

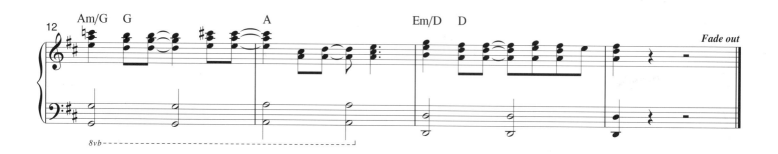

38

# JUST THE WAY YOU ARE

**Words and Music by Billy Joel**

One of the most endearing love songs of Billy Joel's career, "Just the Way You Are" is a classy ballad that deals directly with one of love's greatest features, acceptance. The famous opening line, "Don't go changing to try and please me," leads to the beautiful chorus sentiment "I love you just the way you are," as Joel gives reassurance that his love is heartfelt and everlasting. It is a true song of love, one dedicated at many weddings—and rightfully so. The song was a huge hit for Joel, and is now considered a standard. Its elegant arrangement, including a tasteful sax solo from jazz legend Phil Woods, rolls over a vaguely Latin groove.

**Figure 25—Intro, Verse 1, and Verse 2**

The heavily-chorused Rhodes electric piano that opens the song helps make this intro instantly recognizable. Joel cleverly alternates occurrences of the iv chord (Gm6) with the IV chord (G).

In the verse, Billy uses a variety of jazzy sixth and seventh chords, as well as many ii–V–I progressions (the archetypical jazz standard progression). The major-turning-minor sound of the Gmaj7–Gm7 movement in measures 9–10 harks back to the major/minor duality of the intro. The end of the second verse is slightly different from the first in terms of its harmony (Em7–G/A in meas. 33–34, instead of E9sus–E7–G/A in 17–19). Joel tacks on an ending (not shown) just after the title line that matches the intro.

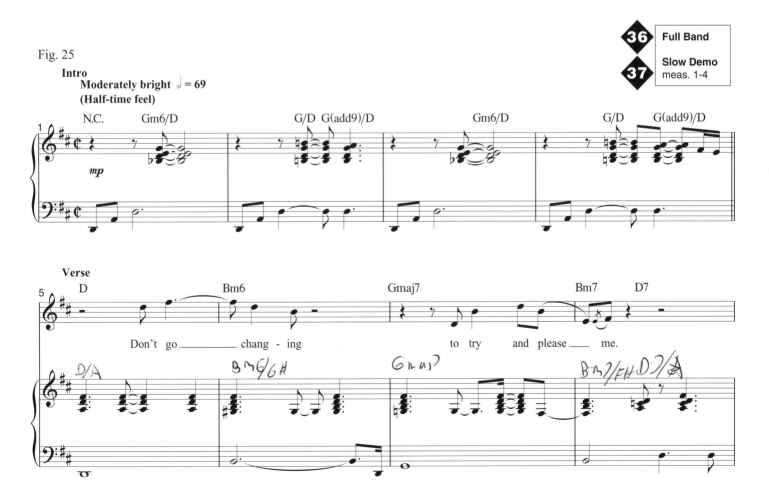

Fig. 25

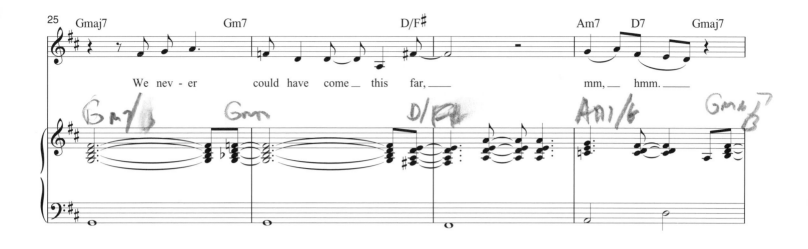

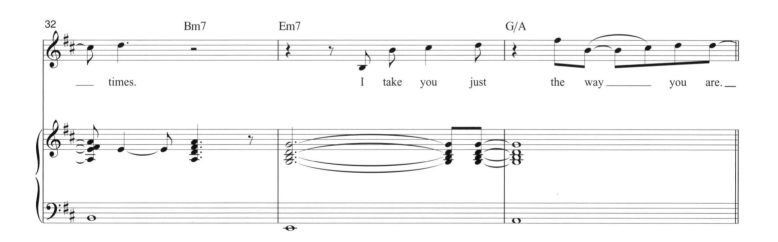

**Figure 26—Bridge**

The bridge is another fine example of the way Billy Joel effortlessly weaves his progressions in and out of different key areas. (Compare this to the bridge in "New York State of Mind.") Notice also how the chords embellish and complement the vocal: In measures 9–10, a descending C chord mirrors the descending vocal melody; in measures 15–16, Joel climbs up four positions of the G/A chord to fill in the break and set up the next verse.

Fig. 26

42

# THE STRANGER

**Words and Music by Billy Joel**

"The Stranger" is an excursion into the secret personalities that we sometimes exude when we are alone or in the throes of passion. Joel gives a psychological dissertation on how we are affected by the parts of ourselves that we hide from even our closest friends and lovers. In the song, he questions whether we realize who we really are, or who even our companions appear to be. The allure of our more primitive side can be strong, though Joel knows that "he isn't always evil and he is not always wrong." Good intentions aside, Joel states "you'll give in to your desire when the stranger comes along," knowing full well that the "stranger" is always a part of who we are. "The Stranger" is a powerful metaphor for our dark sides, and how we wield them.

### Figure 27—Prelude

The instrumental prelude to "The Stranger" can be separated into two parts: the initial eight measures of solo piano, followed by ten measures (the eight-measure theme plus a two-measure ending) under the whistled melody. The harmonies are primarily diatonic, with occasional chromaticism—notably when he tonicizes the Am in measures 5–6 by using the E–D/F♯–G♯dim7, and also when he uses the B/D♯ and B7 chords (from the E harmonic minor scale) in measures 8 and 11. All this adds to the quasi-classical sound of the prelude.

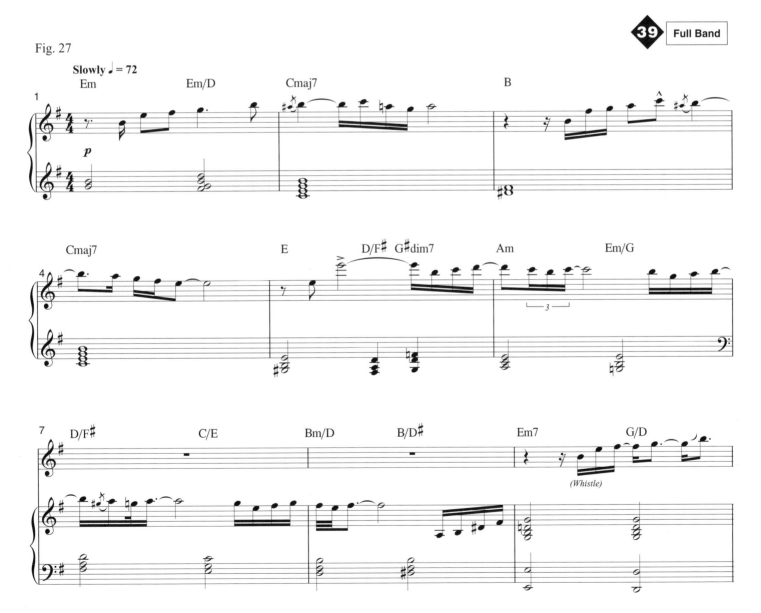

Fig. 27

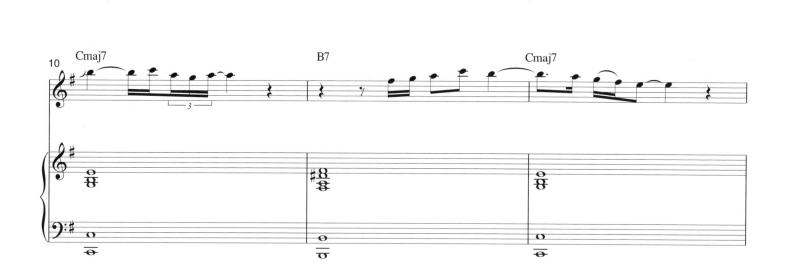

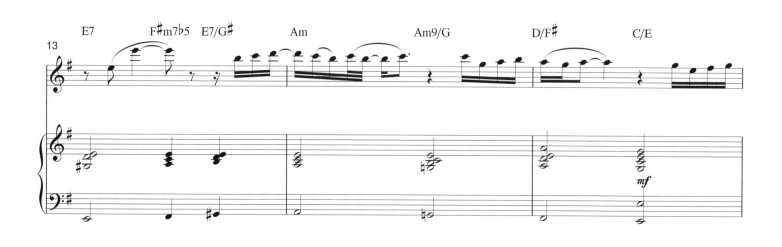

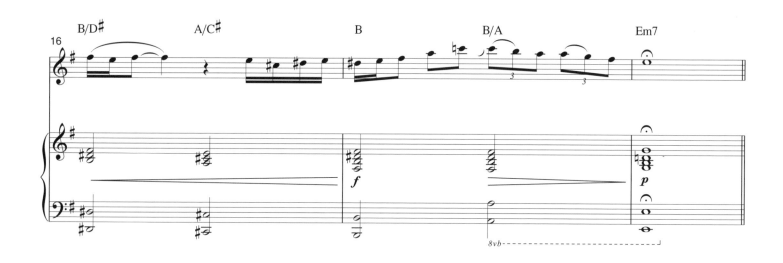

44

# SHE'S ALWAYS A WOMAN

**Words and Music by Billy Joel**

In one of his most tender songs, Joel alternately praises and denounces the woman he loves. By using the ubiquitous "she" instead of a name, Joel writes allegorically of all women, and their effects on the men who love them. In the end he delivers the title sentiment, "but she's always a woman to me." The song sounds romantic, though a quick glance through the lyrics reveals the same disillusionment that other Joel songs like "Stiletto" deliver. "She's Always a Woman" is the polar opposite of the classic ballad "She's Got a Way" in Joel's canon. Ultimately, he takes the blame for all the things he lets her do to him.

### Figure 28—Intro, Verse 1, and Verse 2

Don't let the changing time signatures of 12/8, 9/8, and 6/8 bother you—it's all to accommodate the melody, which has a very natural feel to it. The overall feel is always in three.

The combination of delicate chording, a smooth, flowing melody, and lyrical imagery makes the verses powerfully effective. Beginning in measure 9, note the gentle waves of arpeggios Joel lays down below the vocal as he builds into verse 2—a clear indication of his classical training—plus the addition of jazz master/Joel session-man Steve Khan's acoustic guitar in the second verse.

**40** Full Band

**41** Slow Demo
meas. 9-16

Fig. 28

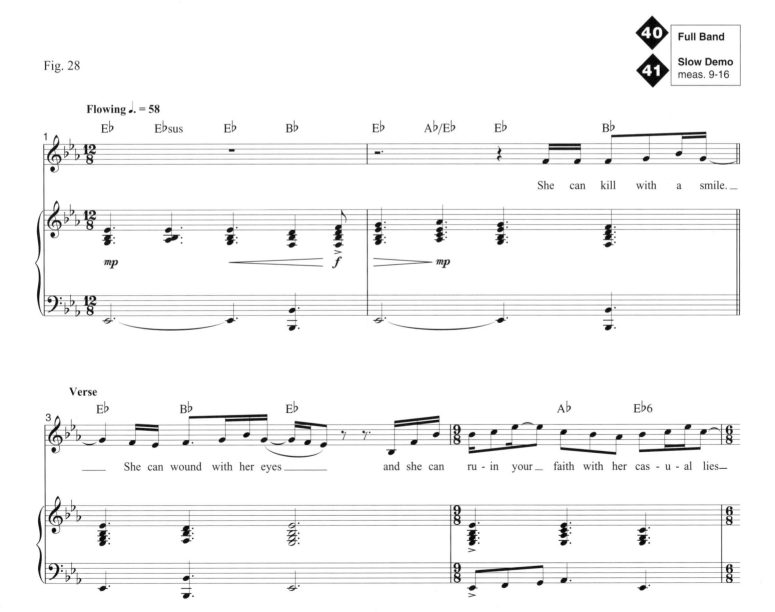

and she on - ly re - veals _ what she wants you to see. _

_ She hides like a child, _ but she's al - ways a wom - an _ to

me. She can lead you to love. _ She can take you or leave you. _ She can

**Verse**

ask for the truth, _ but she'll nev - er be - lieve _____ you and she'll

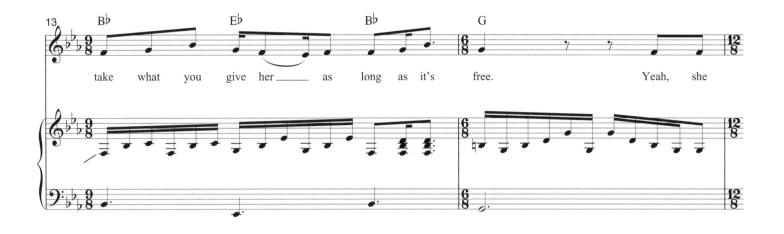

## Figure 29—Bridge

The whole bridge is in 12/8 and begins on Cm, the vi chord, which helps delineate this as a new section. Billy sings at the top of his range to help contrast the bridge with verse. We also hear the familiar Joel device of stepwise, descending bass movement in nearly every measure. The arpeggiated style of playing established in verse 2 continues throughout the rest of the song.

Fig. 29

**Bridge**

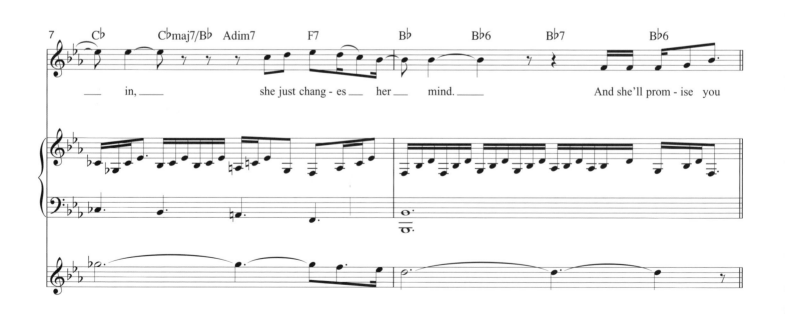

# SCENES FROM AN ITALIAN RESTAURANT

**Words and Music by Billy Joel**

"Scenes from an Italian Restaurant" is one of Billy Joel's epic "story" songs, falling in line with "The Ballad of Billy The Kid" and "Miami 2017" as a multi-movement work using many characters and a stretching timeline. This song uses flashbacks to reminisce about the old neighborhood and the gang over a couple of bottles of wine at the Italian bistro in the title. Joel's vivid memories of his "sweet romantic teenage nights" lead to a vignette about Brenda and Eddie, the "popular steadies" whose changing lives are symbolic of their class and generation.

**Figure 30—Intro and Verse 1**

Joel introduces the song with simple chords in F. At the beginning of the verse, he helps establish the Italian restaurant vibe with the addition of an accordion sound. He continues comping on piano throughout and fills in between vocal phrases.

**44** Full Band

**45** Slow Demos: meas. 1-4, 8

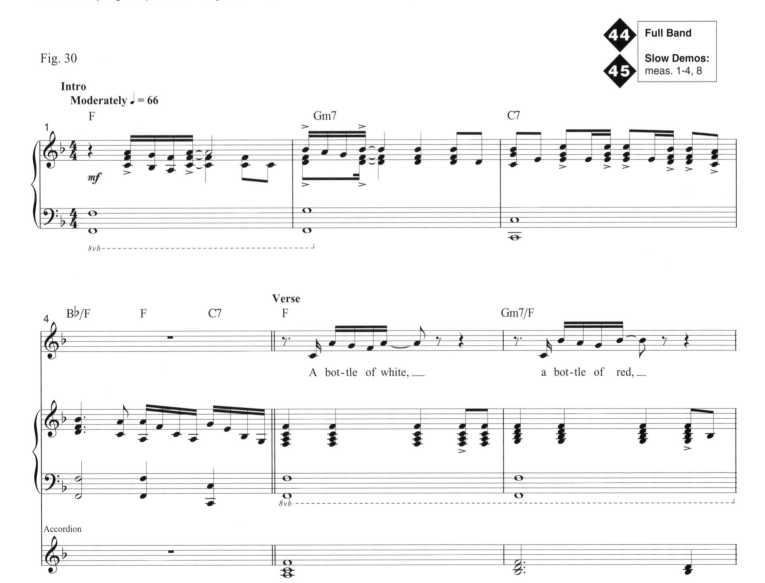

## Figure 31—Piano Solo, Interlude, and Verse 4

The piano solo begins with a left-hand octave pattern in 16th notes. In measure 3, Joel plays some 32nd- and 16th-note flourishes. Listen to the solo demo of this first, and practice it slowly before attempting it at tempo.

Joel continues his 16th-note left-hand patter during the interlude and verse and adds syncopated chords in the right.

# BIG SHOT
## Words and Music by Billy Joel

In one of Billy Joel's most vicious songs, he cuts down a NYC socialite who evidently made a fool of herself while under the influence. Joel's scathing commentary on the jet-set crowd rings true as he tells the "big shot" in question about her embarrassing behavior at some uptown party the night before, and rips into her for going "over the line" and making a fool of herself. This is a classic Joel hit, and his sneering vocals deliver the song's message perfectly.

**Figure 32—Intro and Verse 1**

"Big Shot" is in the key of C major, but it starts out feeling very much like E minor due to the way the chords are used. Notice that the intro begins in bass clef, as the low piano doubles the classic guitar riff that starts the song. The first four measures go through the Em7sus–G riff twice, with hits on the "and" of beats 1 and 3 in measure 4. The Bm chord (over a D bass note) in measure 6 works very well as a link from Em to C.

A repeated Em(sus) chord in measure 8 leads into the verse, which continues along the same basic chord progression as the intro. Notice how the notes D and A are suspended throughout the dark verse chords, until the release on measures 15–16 with the C and F/C.

Fig. 32

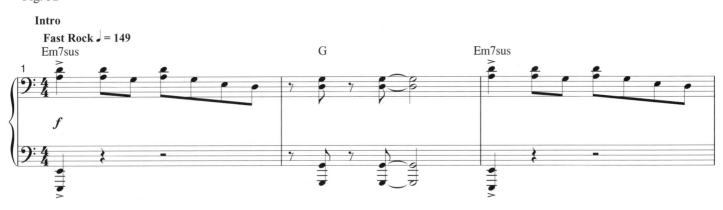

**Figure 33—Chorus**

Again, a repeated eighth-note chord—this time G major—sets up the chorus. The chorus chords are diatonic, from the C major scale, and stick with the IV, V, and vi (F, G, and Am). The bass line in the left hand, however, is on a different track melodically and rhythmically, and its movement gives the song impetus. In the first four measures, Joel sticks to F and C in the bass, using them in relation to the G and F chords on top to create a Lydian-type sound. In measures 6–8, the bass line moves up a whole step to G and D, similarly bouncing back and forth below the same chords on top and brightening things up in the process. Transitional C–E bass-note punches in measure 9 lead back into the cycle, until the big release in measures 14–17, a legato chord movement setting up the return to the intro riff.

Fig. 33

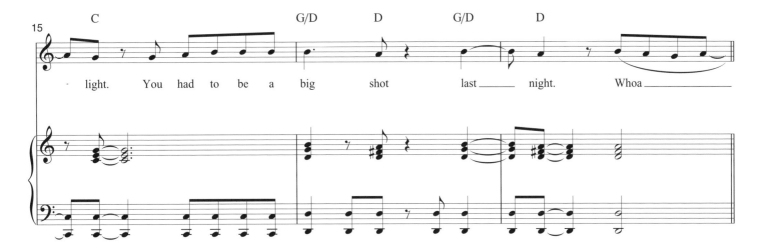

## Figure 34—Bridge

The second time through the chorus leads to the bridge. The bass notes arpeggiate the notes of the chords above them, such as F–A–C under the F chord in measure 1. When one writes on piano, those climbing left-hand octaves are very natural, especially in rock 'n' roll. The main chords follow a "cycle of fifths" progression pounded in straight eighths: F–C–G–D.

Fig. 34

**50** Full Band

**51** Slow Demo: meas. 1-4

# HONESTY

**Words and Music by Billy Joel**

"Honesty" is one of Joel's "moral of the story" songs, touching on a subject with which everyone struggles at some point or another. Joel switches back and forth from second to first person in his exploration of truth and communication, searching for sincerity from others while alluding to the false security that empty promises and sympathy bring only temporarily. In the chorus, he tells us that "everyone is so untrue," but that the honesty he really needs is not from everyone in the world, but from his lover. The song's delicate feel and descending and rising chord progressions mirror this sentiment.

**Figure 35—Intro, Verse, and Chorus**

"Honesty" is in B♭ Major, but Joel clearly begins in B♭ minor, only moving toward the major after the F7 is struck in measure 2. During the verse, he plays primarily diatonic chords in a simple quarter-note rhythm. Just before the chorus he plays a ii–V in G— only to resolve to E♭, a deceptive resolution that is sometimes heard in the key of G minor.

In the chorus, Joel seems centered in G minor, partly due to the strong D/F♯–Gm resolutions, and also because of the prominent D7s (V of Gm), even though they invariably resolve deceptively to E♭.

Fig. 35

# MY LIFE

**Words and Music by Billy Joel**

One of Billy Joel's biggest hits, the upbeat pop song "My Life" is a manifesto to independence, delivered succinctly with the chorus line "I don't care what you say anymore, this is my life. Go ahead with your own life. Leave me alone." This is a gentle kiss-off to parents, or perhaps a controlling lover, and Joel gets his point across without anger or negativity. Much of the song is written in the first person, as Joel speaks directly to his oppressor, using terms like "I don't want you to tell me..." or "I don't care what you say..." as he leads to the uncompromising "you can speak your mind, but not on my time." Surely many people were inspired by this song to stand for what they believe in, and discount the sometimes ill-stated opinions of others.

### Figure 36—Intro, Interlude, and Verse

"My Life" begins with a grooving introduction consisting of simple chords over a D pedal point. But before long, Joel reaches outside the key for some added color, particularly during the interlude, where nearly all the chords are borrowed—D9, C9, E♭maj7/F, F7, and B♭.

Joel uses a chromatic, disco-style (no one was really immune to disco fever in '78) walk-up in measure 16 to set up the verse, which is firmly rooted back in D major.

Fig. 36

53 **Full Band**

54 **Slow Demo:** meas. 13-16

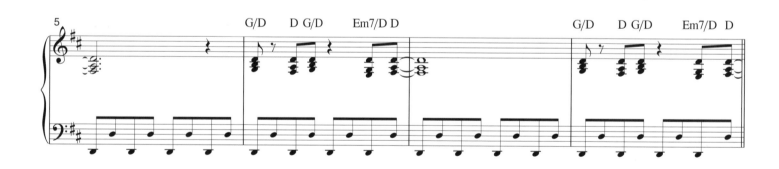

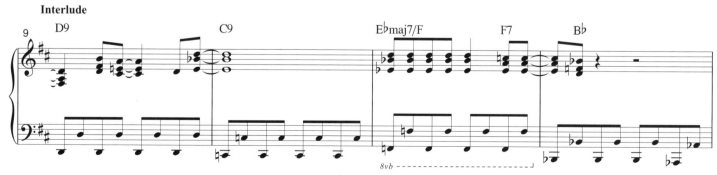

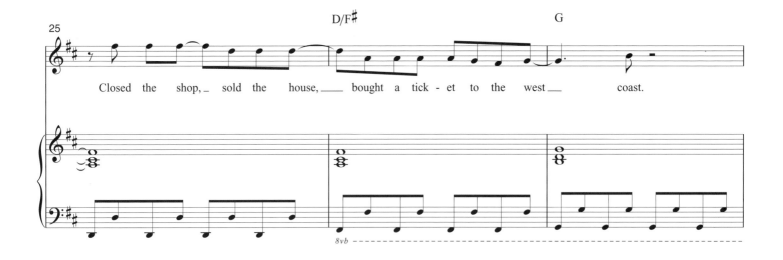

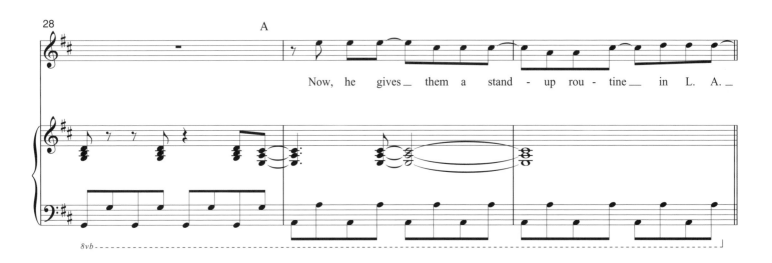

## Figure 37—Bridge

After a chorus that is identical to the verse, the bridge begins on the vi chord (Bm) and then moves to the emotional F♯7/C♯ chord, the V of Bm. If we've learned anything about Joel's bridges so far, it's that they are predictable in their unpredictability. This V chord resolves deceptively to a string of dominant chords before finally moving back to Bm and, lastly, toward the V (the G/A and A) of our tonic key of D.

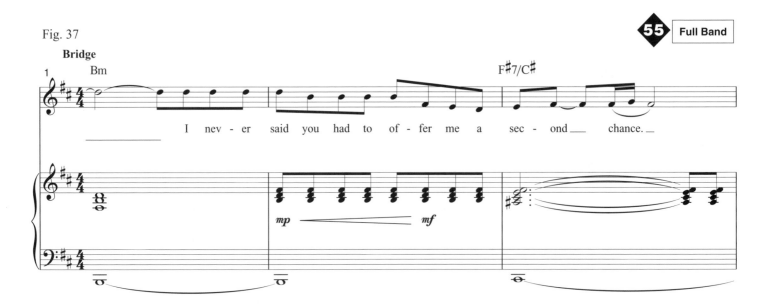

# DON'T ASK ME WHY

**Words and Music by Billy Joel**

"Don't Ask Me Why" stands out a bit in the Joel catalog due to the Latin-influenced rhythmic feel, drifting somewhere north of a Samba. The song uses nice symbolism in its lyrics as Joel addresses someone who is putting on airs but is "no stranger to the street." He slyly intimates that although the person addressed has everyone fooled with fashion and style, he knows that it's all an act. However, as the title plainly states, he doesn't profess to having the answers, and remains rather casual and uninvolved in his lyrical observations.

### Figure 38—Intro, Verse, and Chorus

This song is in the key of B♭ and is played in *cut time* (2/2) throughout. The intro is six measures long, and follows a repetitive pattern of I–IV/I chords.

Joel focuses on small phrases throughout the song, and as such, the sections don't wind up being clean eight- and sixteen-measure lengths. So we have six-measure intros, fourteen-measure verses, etc.

One notable thing that Joel does here is create little three-chord patterns that last one measure each and get repeated symmetrically in a larger pattern. That larger pattern is in the lyrics; the first three lines total twelve measures—four to each pattern—and the last line is only two measures long. In each four-measure line is an order of little one-measure patterns, each of which has an ascending bass line, though the first and third chords are the same. This occurs in measures 7–8 with B♭–Cm7–B♭/D, then again in measure 9 with C–Dm7–C7/E. Notice how each line follows basically the same chord progression in a different range. This is a good example of many different levels of patterns within the larger chord progression; you have the one-measure pattern, the four-measure pattern, and the twelve- or sixteen-measure progression too. Having this multi-level vision will help you to understand the song.

The verses overlap the choruses with the melodic resolve, so that the return to the tonic coincides with the first bar of the chorus.

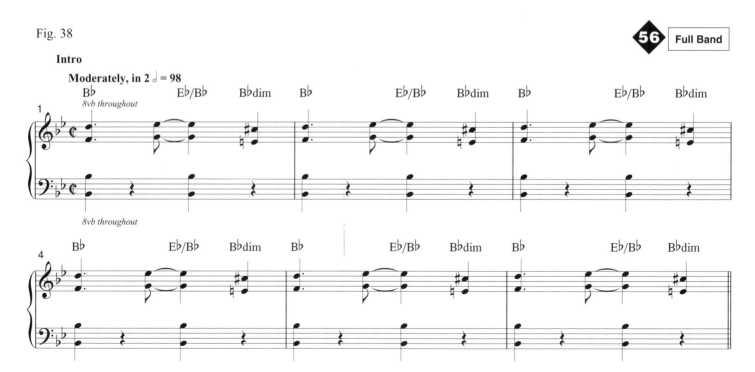

Fig. 38

56 Full Band

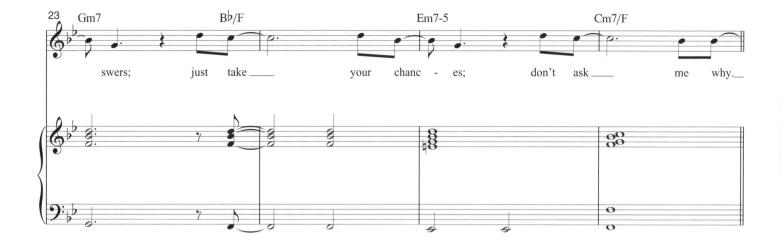

**Figure 39—Bridge**

This is a simple four-line bridge, with each line lasting four measures. Note how Joel returns to the tonic (B♭ major) on beat 4 of the pickup measure, to accommodate this spacious release from the relatively busy verse and chorus patterns.

The first half of the bridge sticks with the IV and V chords and holds off on the resolution to the I until measure 7. The second half is more adventurous, moving up to the key of C, if only temporarily, and eventually cycling through dominant chords leading back to B♭.

Fig. 39

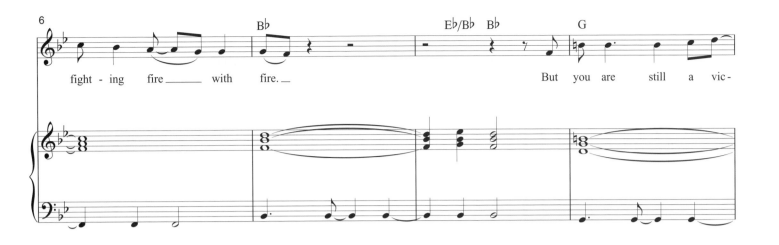

fight - ing fire ___ with fire. ___ But you are still a vic-

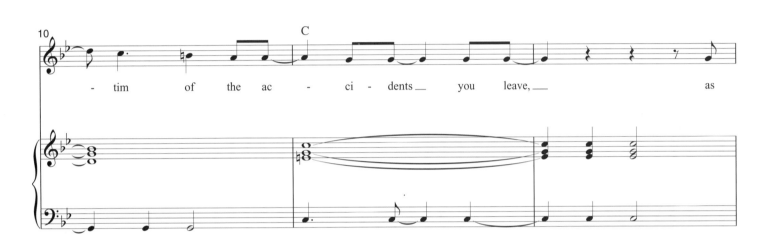

-tim of the ac - ci - dents ___ you leave, ___ as

sure as I'm a vic - tim of ___ de - si - yi - yi - re.

## Figure 40—Interlude (Piano Solo)

After a third verse and chorus comes a brief piano solo, played over a slightly altered bridge progression. Joel's tasteful solo begins with a glissando up to the F chord, over which he begins a series of octave/third figures that follow the chord changes. Quarter-note triplets add to the Latin jazz flavor, as does the tremolo in measures 11–12. (Alternate between the upper G/E♭ notes with two right-hand fingers, while holding the lower G on the left hand.) A series of two-handed octave runs follows, ending with a chromatic flurry in measure 16 that begins on F and leads to the tonic B♭ at the start of the last verse.

**58** Full Band

**59** Slow Demo: meas. 1-16

Fig. 40

# KEYBOARD *signature licks*

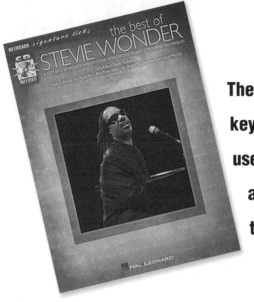

These exceptional book/CD packs teach keyboardists the techniques and styles used by popular artists from yesterday and today. Each folio breaks down the trademark riffs and licks used by these great performers.

## BEST OF BEBOP PIANO
*by Gene Rizzo*
16 bebop piano transcriptions: April in Paris • Between the Devil and the Deep Blue Sea • I Don't Stand a Ghost of a Chance • If I Were a Bell • Lullaby of Birdland • On a Clear Day (You Can See Forever) • Satin Doll • Thou Swell • and more.
00695734 .................................................................................$22.95

## BILL EVANS
*by Brent Edstrom*
12 songs from pianist Bill Evans, including: Five • One for Helen • The Opener • Peace Piece • Peri's Scope • Quiet Now • Re: Person I Knew • Time Remembered • Turn Out the Stars • Very Early • Waltz for Debby • 34 Skidoo.
00695714 .................................................................................$22.95

## BEN FOLDS FIVE
*by Todd Lowry*
16 songs from four Ben Folds Five albums: Alice Childress • Battle of Who Could Care Less • Boxing • Brick • Don't Change Your Plans • Evaporated • Kate • The Last Polka • Lullabye • Magic • Narcolepsy • Philosophy • Song for the Dumped • Underground.
00695578 .................................................................................$22.95

## BILLY JOEL CLASSICS: 1974-1980
*by Robbie Gennet*
15 popular hits from the '70s by Billy Joel: Big Shot • Captain Jack • Don't Ask Me Why • The Entertainer • Honesty • Just the Way You Are • Movin' Out (Anthony's Song) • My Life • New York State of Mind • Piano Man • Root Beer Rag • Say Goodbye to Hollywood • Scenes from an Italian Restaurant • She's Always a Woman • The Stranger.
00695581 .................................................................................$22.95

## BILLY JOEL HITS: 1981-1993
*by Todd Lowry*
15 more hits from Billy Joel in the '80s and '90s: All About Soul • Allentown • And So It Goes • Baby Grand • I Go to Extremes • Leningrad • Lullabye (Goodnight, My Angel) • Modern Woman • Pressure • The River of Dreams • She's Got a Way • Tell Her About It • This Is the Time • Uptown Girl • You're Only Human (Second Wind).
00695582 .................................................................................$22.95

## ELTON JOHN CLASSIC HITS
*by Todd Lowry*
10 of Elton's best are presented in this book/CD pack: Blue Eyes • Chloe • Don't Go Breaking My Heart • Don't Let the Sun Go Down on Me • Ego • I Guess That's Why They Call It the Blues • Little Jeannie • Sad Songs (Say So Much) • Someone Saved My Life Tonight • Sorry Seems to Be the Hardest Word.
00695688 .................................................................................$22.95

## LENNON & McCARTNEY HITS
*by Todd Lowry*
Features 15 hits from A-L for keyboard by the legendary songwriting team of John Lennon and Paul McCartney. Songs include: All You Need Is Love • Back in the U.S.S.R. • The Ballad of John and Yoko • Because • Birthday • Come Together • A Day in the Life • Don't Let Me Down • Drive My Car • Get Back • Good Day Sunshine • Hello, Goodbye • Hey Jude • In My Life • Lady Madonna.
00695650 .................................................................................$22.95

## LENNON & McCARTNEY FAVORITES
*by Todd Lowry*
16 more hits (L-Z) from this songwriting duo from The Beatles: Let It Be • The Long and Winding Road • Lucy in the Sky with Diamonds • Martha My Dear • Ob-La-Di, Ob-La-Da • Oh! Darling • Penny Lane • Revolution 9 • Rocky Raccoon • She's a Woman • Strawberry Fields Forever • We Can Work It Out • With a Little Help from My Friends • The Word • You're Going to Lose That Girl • Your Mother Should Know.
00695651 .................................................................................$22.95

## BEST OF ROCK 'N' ROLL PIANO
*by David Bennett Cohen*
12 of the best hits for piano are presented in this pack. Songs include: At the Hop • Blueberry Hill • Brown-Eyed Handsome Man • Charlie Brown • Great Balls of Fire • Jailhouse Rock • Lucille • Rock and Roll Is Here to Stay • Runaway • Tutti Frutti • Yakety Yak • You Never Can Tell.
00695627 .................................................................................$19.95

## BEST OF STEVIE WONDER
*by Todd Lowry*
This book/CD pack includes musical examples, lessons, biographical notes, and more for 14 of Stevie Wonder's best songs. Features: I Just Called to Say I Love You • My Cherie Amour • Part Time Lover • Sir Duke • Superstition • You Are the Sunshine of My Life • and more.
00695605 .................................................................................$22.95

Prices, contents and availability subject to change without notice.

0203

# Check out these great Keyboard Recorded Versions from Hal Leonard

0402

# KEYBOARD STYLE SERIES

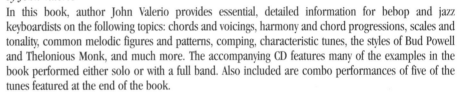

*These book/CD packs provide focused lessons that contain valuable how-to insight, essential playing tips, and beneficial information for all players. Comprehensive treatment is given to each subject, complete with a companion CD, which features many of the examples in the book performed either solo or with a full band.*

## BEBOP JAZZ PIANO
THE COMPLETE GUIDE
*by John Valerio*

In this book, author John Valerio provides essential, detailed information for bebop and jazz keyboardists on the following topics: chords and voicings, harmony and chord progressions, scales and tonality, common melodic figures and patterns, comping, characteristic tunes, the styles of Bud Powell and Thelonious Monk, and much more. The accompanying CD features many of the examples in the book performed either solo or with a full band. Also included are combo performances of five of the tunes featured at the end of the book.
00290535 Book/CD Pack......................................................................................................$16.95

## ROCK KEYBOARDS
THE COMPLETE GUIDE
*by Scott Miller*

*Rock Keyboard* is chock full of authentic rock keyboard parts. Learn to comp or solo in any of your favorite rock styles. Listen to the CD to hear your parts fit in with the total groove of the band. Includes 99 tracks! Covers: classic rock, pop/rock, blues rock, Southern rock, hard rock, progressive rock, alternative rock, and heavy metal.
00310823 Book/CD Pack......................................................................................................$14.95

## ROCK & ROLL PIANO
THE COMPLETE GUIDE
*by Andy Vinter*

With this pack, you'll learn the skills you need to take your place alongside Fats Domino, Jerry Lee Lewis, Little Richard, and other great rock 'n' roll piano players of the '50s and '60s! CD includes demos and backing tracks so you can play along with every example. Also includes six complete tunes at the end of the book! Covers: left-hand patterns; basic rock 'n' roll progressions; right-hand techniques; straight eighths vs. swing eighths; glisses, crushed notes, rolls, note clusters, and more; how to solo; influential players, styles and recordings; and much more!
00310912 Book/CD Pack......................................................................................................$14.95

## STRIDE & SWING PIANO
THE COMPLETE GUIDE
*by John Valerio*

Learn the styles of the masters of stride and swing piano, such as Scott Joplin, Jimmy Yancey, Pete Johnson, Jelly Roll Morton, James P. Johnson, Fats Waller, Teddy Wilson, and Art Tatum. This pack covers classic ragtime, early blues and boogie woogie, New Orleans jazz, and more, and includes 14 full songs.
00310882 Book/CD Pack......................................................................................................$16.95

Prices, contents, and availability subject to change without notice.

FOR MORE INFORMATION, SEE YOUR LOCAL MUSIC DEALER,
OR WRITE TO:

HAL•LEONARD®
CORPORATION
7777 W. BLUEMOUND RD. P.O. BOX 13819 MILWAUKEE, WI 53213

Visit Hal Leonard online at
**www.halleonard.com**